MILWAUKEE ROAD
1850 THROUGH 1960

PHOTO ARCHIVE

MILWAUKEE ROAD 1850 THROUGH 1960

PHOTO ARCHIVE

Photographs from
The State Historical Society of Wisconsin

Edited with introduction by
P.A. Letourneau

Iconografix
Photo Archive Series

Iconografix
PO Box 609
Osceola, Wisconsin 54020 USA

Library of Congress Card Number 96-76223

ISBN 1-882256-61-1

96 97 98 99 00 5 4 3 2 1

Cover design by Lou Gordon, Osceola, Wisconsin

Printed in the United States of America

Book trade distribution by Voyageur Press, Inc. (800) 888-9653

PREFACE

The histories of machines and mechanical gadgets are contained in the books, journals, correspondence, and personal papers stored in libraries and archives throughout the world. Written in tens of languages, covering thousands of subjects, the stories are recorded in millions of words.

Words are powerful. Yet, the impact of a single image, a photograph or an illustration, often relates more than dozens of pages of text. Fortunately, many of the libraries and archives that house the words also preserve the images.

In the *Photo Archive Series,* Iconografix reproduces photographs and illustrations selected from public and private collections. The images are chosen to tell a story—to capture the character of their subject. Reproduced as found, they are accompanied by the captions made available by the archive.

The Iconografix *Photo Archive Series* is dedicated to young and old alike, the enthusiast, the collector and anyone who, like us, is fascinated by "things" mechanical.

A class F7 Hudson on the point of the *Hiawatha*, 1939.

INTRODUCTION

The Milwaukee Road began as the Milwaukee and Waukesha Rail Road in 1847. The original charter proposed a 20 mile route, but by 1849 it was revised to allow service to Madison, the Wisconsin state capital, and beyond to the Mississippi River, which defined a portion of Wisconsin's western border with the Minnesota Territory.

The first five mile section of track was operational in November 1850, by which time the road's name had been changed to the Milwaukee and Mississippi Rail Road. The line between Milwaukee and Waukesha was completed in February 1851. Madison was reached by 1854; the Mississippi at Prairie du Chien by 1857; and the road's first brush with extinction by 1860. In 1861, following voluntary foreclosure, the road was sold to East Coast interests and was renamed the Milwaukee and Prairie du Chien Railway. In 1867, the Milwaukee and Prairie du Chien was absorbed by the Milwaukee and St. Paul Railway, and control was returned to Wisconsin interests. The Milwaukee and St. Paul acquired the St. Paul and Chicago Railway in 1872. With nearly 1,400 miles of track and terminals in the three principal cities of the Upper Midwest, the system clearly merited redefinition. In 1874, it was renamed The Chicago, Milwaukee and St. Paul Railway Company.

Over the next 30 years, through both the construction of new track and the acquisition of existing railroads, the Chicago, Milwaukee and St. Paul expanded within Wisconsin, Illinois, Minnesota, and Iowa. It entered the Dakotas and

Missouri, adding terminals at Fargo in 1885 and Kansas City in 1887. By 1890, the company had reached an agreement with the Union Pacific that brought the Chicago, Milwaukee and St. Paul across the Missouri River from Council Bluffs, Iowa to Omaha's Union Station; it purchased the Milwaukee and Northern Railroad Company and thereby gained access to Michigan's iron-rich Upper Peninsula. By 1890, the Chicago, Milwaukee and St. Paul operated in eight states, and total track miles stood at just over 7,000, an impressive 400 percent increase since 1874.

The next significant spurt in the company's growth followed the decision to expand to the Northwest on a route from South Dakota to Seattle and Tacoma, Washington. In October 1905, the Chicago, Milwaukee and St. Paul Railway Company of Washington was incorporated as The Pacific Railway Company, and construction of the line was begun from Mobridge, South Dakota in the spring of 1906. Completed in less than three years, at a cost exceeding $230 million, the expansion west added more than 2,300 miles to the Milwaukee Road, traversing western South Dakota, Montana, Idaho, and Washington. The electrification of 650 miles of the route, begun in 1914, cost another $23 million.

The road west was financed through the sale of long-term bonds. The burden of this debt would eventually bankrupt the Milwaukee Road, although it was not the sole reason for its failure. In 1925, the Chicago, Milwaukee and St. Paul Railway Company was forced into receivership. Reorganized under the control of National City Bank of New York and the investment bank of Kuhn, Loeb & Company, it operated in receivership until 1928, when the newly formed Chicago, Milwaukee, St. Paul and Pacific Railroad Company purchased its assets. This company, too, would fail in June 1935, a victim of decreased revenues during the Great Depression. Reorganization moved slowly through the maze of private interests—the stock and bond holders and creditors—and the Interstate Commerce Commission's bureaucracy. No reorganization plan had been accepted by the time the US entered World War II. Throughout the war, the Milwaukee Road continued to operate and, as did most US railroads, prospered. A reorganization plan was finally approved in 1944 and the company emerged from bankruptcy in early 1945.

The Milwaukee Road celebrated its 100th anniversary in 1948, amidst the sense of post-war optimism that had infected all of America. It was a time of rebuilding and refitting at the Milwaukee Road, as rationing of materials during the war had delayed replacement of equipment. A national shortage of freight cars kept the Milwaukee's car-building shops working overtime. The changeover from steam to diesel required significant investments in locomotives and maintenance facilities. All this during a period of declining traffic, as airlines, personal automobiles, and interstate truck lines attracted an ever-increasing amount of passengers and freight. Sadly, the Milwaukee Road never regained the momentum it had maintained throughout much of its history. By 1960, the final year covered by this book, the Milwaukee's glory days lay only its past.

The photographs in *Milwaukee Road 1850 through 1960 Photo Archive* were selected from the collection of The State Historical Society of Wisconsin. An effort was made to include a variety of photographs, depicting steam, electric, and diesel locomotives, train crews, construction workers, shop employees, and various facilities. However, many aspects of the Milwaukee's history could not be documented, as the Society's collection is by no means comprehensive. Nonetheless, as is evidenced by this volume, the collection is an impressive and valuable record of one of America's greatest railroads.

Bob Ellis, locomotive No. 71, built by Norris Works, Pennsylvania in 1848. Operated by the Milwaukee & Mississippi Railroad, it was the first locomotive on the Milwaukee Road. This photograph was retouched: drive wheels, side rods, engine truck, cab headlight brackets, smoke stack, pilot beam, and the entire tender are not original.

D.A. Olin, a wood-burner built in 1854 and one of the first locomotives of the Milwaukee & St. Paul line. It would later be renumbered 42.

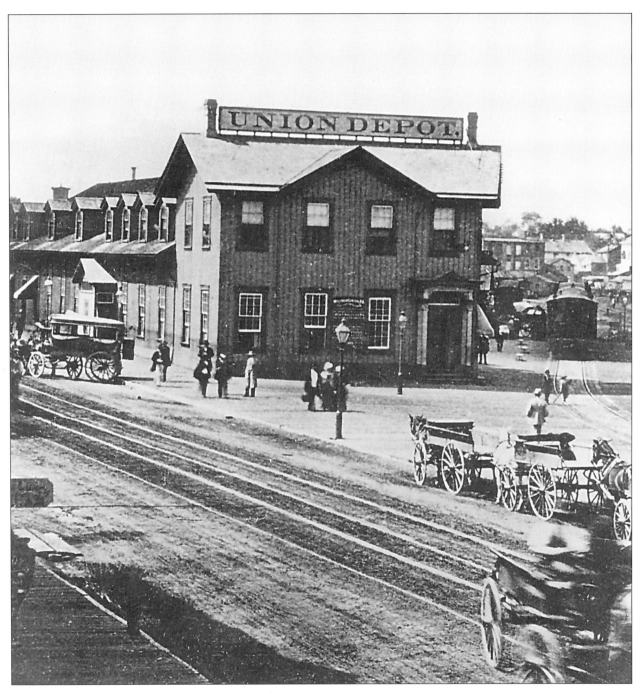

Milwaukee Union Depot,
built in 1866, circa 1870.

L.B. Rock, Milwaukee & St. Paul No. 40, built at the Chestnut Street yards in 1854. Photographed at Milwaukee in 1869.

A locomotive of the Pine River Valley & Stevens Point Railway in transit from Lone Rock to Richland Center, Wisconsin, March 1876. In 1880, this line was sold to the Chicago, Milwaukee & St. Paul.

An unidentified CM&StP wood-burner at Kilbourn, Wisconsin, 1878.

The locomotive *Messenger* with the pay car *Old Peggy,* circa 1880.

No. 75, built in 1850 by Schenectady Locomotive Works, photographed at Winneconne, Wisconsin, 1879.

The Chicago, Milwaukee & St. Paul Milwaukee shops, 1883.

J.H. Benedict, locomotive No. 142 built by Danforth and Cook in 1869, at the depot in Tomahawk, Wisconsin, 1885.

Locomotive No. 367, built in 1880 by Schenectady Locomotive Works, photographed at Milwaukee, 1884.

Locomotive No. 216, built in 1878 by Baldwin Locomotive Works, photographed in the Reed Street yards, Milwaukee, 1886.

Shop men at the terminal roundhouse, Madison, Wisconsin.

The car shop and employees, Milwaukee, July 1884.

Locomotive No. 632, class H7 built in 1883 by Rhode Island Locomotive Works, photographed in 1886.

Construction on the line near Red Wing, Minnesota, 1886.

Switch engine No. 312, a class J2 coal-burner built by Rogers Locomotive in 1881, photographed at Milwaukee in 1886.

The general offices in the Mitchell Building, Milwaukee, 1887.

The Old Wood Train, No. 425 built in 1875 by the Manchester Locomotive Works, photographed at Hartford, Wisconsin, 1887.

E.B. Wakeman, No. 21 built in 1857 by Mason Machine Works. The first passenger train to arrive at West Merrill, Wisconsin, 1886.

No. 246, class J2 built by Rogers Locomotive and Machine Works in 1879, photographed at Prairie du Chien, Wisconsin, 1889.

D.L. Bush, built by Niles Locomotive in 1855. Acquired by CM&StP through the 1879 purchase of the Western Union Railroad, Racine, Wisconsin. Photographed in Racine, circa 1885.

Locomotive No. 240, class H5 built in 1879 by Rhode Island Locomotive Works, photographed at Mineral Point, Wisconsin, 1890.

Train No. 8 with No. 359, class H4 locomotive built by Schenectady Locomotive Works in 1880, photographed at North Prairie, Wisconsin in 1897.

H.C. Atkins, No. 80 built in 1870 by the Milwaukee & St. Paul. A runaway with exploded boiler, photographed at Preston, Iowa, circa 1892.

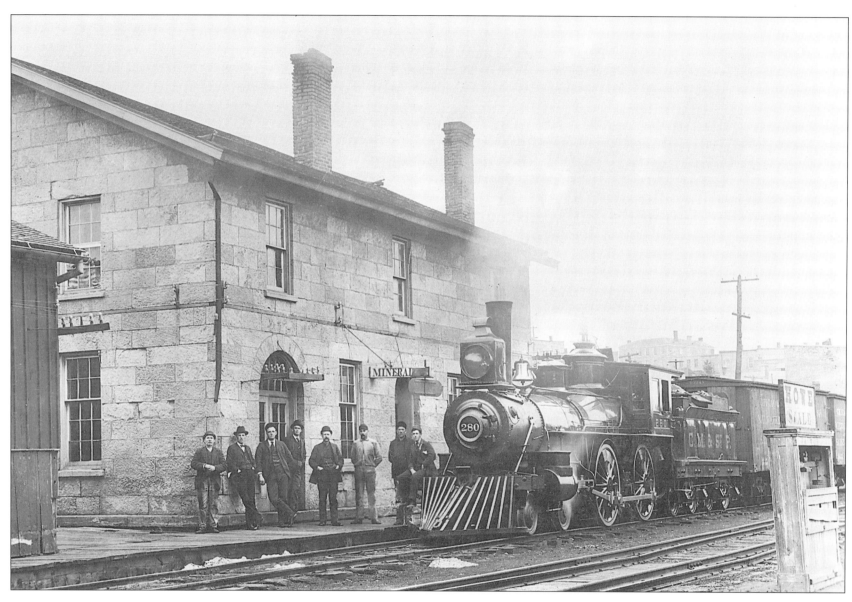

Locomotive No. 280, built in 1873 by Grant Locomotive Works and originally owned by Western Union Railroad, photographed at Mineral Point, Wisconsin, 1890.

No. 280 photographed at Madison, Wisconsin, 1896.

Pullman sleeper *Pioneer* used by CM&StP in 1891.

Interior of the *Pioneer*.

James Toleman, built by Leslie and Company, Ltd. (UK) and exhibited at the 1893 World's Columbian Exposition in Chicago. Brought to Milwaukee for a demonstration, it proved too heavy for use on the CM&StP.

Kilbourn bridge construction.

Promoted as "the largest shipment of boxes ever made," this 30 car train carried 90,000 egg cases valued at $9,000. Pulled by No. 328, built in 1869 by Schenectady Locomotive Works, the train left Wausau, Wisconsin for Indianapolis, Indiana via Milwaukee on January 16, 1896.

No. 939, built by Brooks Locomotive in 1890 and previously No. 39 on the Milwaukee & Northern, photographed at Elkhart Lake, Wisconsin, 1894.

CM&StP employees and wives at Toronto, Iowa, 1895.

No. 827, built in 1892 by Baldwin Locomotive Works, photographed in 1895.

No. 212, built in 1877 by Brooks Locomotive, photographed circa 1890.

Locomotive No. 247, class J2 built by Rogers Locomotive in 1879, photographed in 1897.

Locomotive No. 916, built by Baldwin Locomotive in 1871 and originally owned by the Milwaukee & Northern, operated on the Super Division in 1897.

Locomotive No. 183, built in 1873 by Grant Locomotive Works, photographed circa 1895.

The wreck of CM&StP No. 826 and No. 831, Beaver Dam, Wisconsin, February 10, 1899.

Draw Bridge Z-6 spanned the Chicago River, photographed circa 1900. The high ball signal, installed in 1882, was taken out of service in 1939.

CM&StP employees on an outing near Minocqua, Wisconsin, circa 1890.

No. 1100, switch engine built by Baldwin Locomotive in 1873, originally *Stephen Clement* No. 199. Photographed at Milwaukee in 1903.

A CM&StP train crosses the Menominee River at Iron Mountain, Michigan, circa 1900.

Locomotive No. 1177, class I5 switch engine built in the company shops in 1904 and photographed at Milwaukee in 1906.

The wreck of a narrow gauge train at Zwingle, Iowa, February 1907.

Snowbound on the East High Line, 1909.

The cook crew prepared food in a boxcar kitchen for the men that laid track near Mobridge, South Dakota.

Construction of Tunnel 32 on the extension of the North Fork Line, Idaho, 1908.

Construction on the extension of the North Fork Line, Idaho, 1908.

Bridge construction crew working on the North Fork Line, Idaho, 1908.

Ashland, Wisconsin, 1910.

The Chicago, Milwaukee & St. Paul depot at Babcock, Wisconsin, 1910.

No. 713, class H5-a built in 1883 by Baldwin Locomotive, and crew at Gleason, Wisconsin, 1909.

No. 122 in the Bitter Root Mountains, Montana, circa 1910.

No. 337, built at the Milwaukee shops in 1893 and used around Chicago for suburban passenger and mixed trains. Photographed at Chicago in 1913.

No. 1532, class I5 switch engine built in the company shops in 1908, photographed at Milwaukee in 1914.

Construction and electrification of the Pacific extension. Montana, circa 1917.

Construction and electrification of the Pacific extension. Montana, circa 1917.

Electrification crews at work in Montana. Self-propelled passenger cars were modified for use in line construction.

Electrification crews at work in Montana.

The CM&StP depot at Three Forks, Montana.

General Electric class EF-1 freight motor 10200A & B entered service in 1915.

GE Bipolar Gearless Type No. 10254 entered service in 1919. Photographed with officials of the company in 1920.

No. 10254 leads the *Olympian*, photographed in 1920.

The Western Avenue yards in Chicago, 1917.

CM&StP Milwaukee roundhouse employees, 1917.

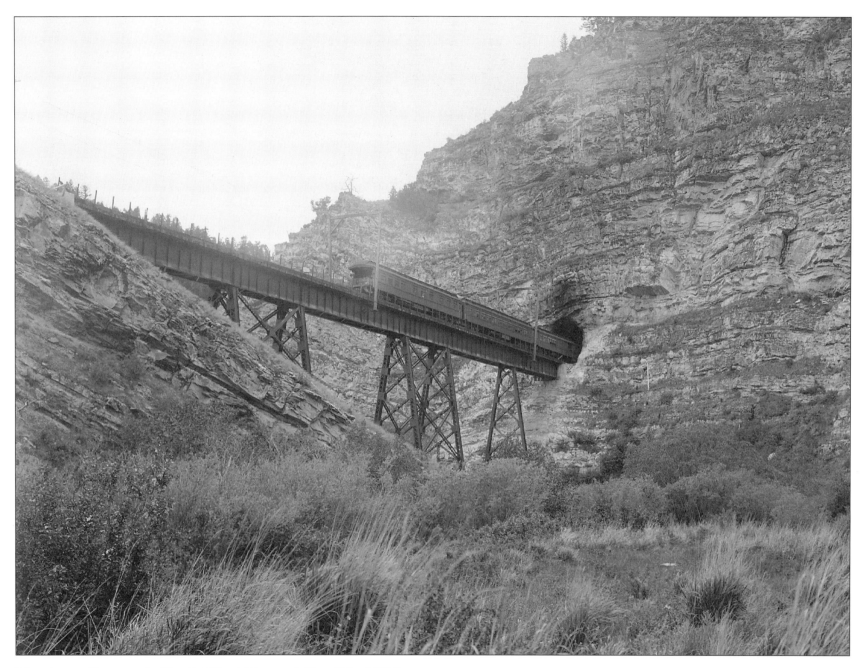

Montana Canyon's Eagle Nest Tunnel No. 33, 1920.

Three views of No. 6414 follow. Built by Baldwin Locomotive Works in 1931, 6414 was one of more than 20 mighty 4-6-4 locomotives purchased by the Chicago, Milwaukee, St. Paul & Pacific in 1930 and 1931. A class F6-a engine, it was renumbered No. 142 in 1938, and was scrapped in 1954.

No. 6414.

No. 6414 was photographed near the shops in Milwaukee. Electric interurbans of The Milwaukee Electric Railway & Light Company (TMER&L) ran under the power line towers.

Locomotive No. 3002, class A1-as built by Baldwin Locomotive in September 1897. Originally No. 840, it was numbered 402 in 1899; 902 in 1901; 3002 in 1912; 21 in 1938, and scrapped in 1940. Photographed May 16, 1931.

No. 8255, class L2-a built by Baldwin Locomotive in 1920, photographed April 28, 1931.

No. 3, built by Birmingham Rail and Locomotive Co. in 1908, photographed at Cascade, Iowa in September 1930.

Locomotive No. 1172, class I5-a switch engine built by CM&StP in 1903, photographed June 8, 1931.

The Milwaukee shops in 1935. *Milwaukee Journal* photo.

No. 2 of the four streamlined class A locomotives built by the American Locomotive Company and introduced into service May 1935. Photographed on May 10, 1935.

No. 2 at the head of the *Hiawatha*, 1935.

The *Hiawatha* arrives at an unknown depot.

No. 3 of the four streamlined class A locomotives built by the American Locomotive Company. Photographed on May 26, 1936.

No. 10, class G (formerly class G6-ps No. 2767), built in the Milwaukee shops in 1900 and streamlined in 1936 to power the *North Woods Hiawatha.* Photographed September 18, 1936.

No. 2767, built by Baldwin Locomotive in 1900 and originally No. 309, photographed at Janesville, Wisconsin in 1937.

No. 206, class S2 built by Baldwin Locomotive in November 1937.

No. 40, a class H8 built by Rogers Locomotive in 1904, photographed in 1939. It entered service as No. 206 on the Chicago, Terre Haute & South Eastern; became No. 900 in 1922; No. 40 in 1938; No. 34 in 1941; No. 97 in 1945, and was scrapped in 1947.

Locomotives No. 177, No. 626, and companions on a siding, circa 1939.

A heavily retouched photograph of an F7 Hudson, 1939.

Class A No. 1 and two F7 Hudsons grace the Milwaukee depot, 1939.

No. 144, class F6-A and originally No. 6416. Built by Baldwin in October 1931. Photographed in 1939.

No. 174, class F3S built by American Locomotive in 1910. It entered service as No. 1515; became No. 3213 in October 1910; No. 6513 in 1912; No. 6133 in 1923; No. 174 in 1938, and was scrapped in 1951.

No. 308, class L3-a and originally No. 8630. Built by American Locomotive in 1918, photographed February 1939.

The *Olympian* pulled by a Bipolar Gearless through the Cascade Mountains, 1939.

No. 151, F-3A Pacific built by American Locomotive in 1910; streamlined in 1941 for *Chippewa Hiawatha* service (Chicago-Milwaukee-Green Bay-Iron Mountain). It entered service as No. 1539; became 3237 in June 1910; 6537 in 1912; 6157 in 1924; 151 in 1938, and was scrapped in 1954. Photographed July 23, 1941.

A company official compares speed tapes from a locomotive with the master tapes. The scale was 1/2-inch to a mile.

The Milwaukee yards, 1940. *Milwaukee Journal* photo.

No. 15, EMD (GM) E6 built in 1941, the first EMD passenger unit on the Milwaukee Road. This unit established a tremendous performance record and, as a result, many EMD locomotives followed.

Interior of a *Hiawatha* observation parlor car with sky-top solar lounge, 1946. The sky-top lounge car was the creation of Brooks Stevens, the noted industrial designer.

No. 990, RSC-2 diesel built by American Locomotive, photographed in 1948 pulling the *North Woods Hiawatha.*

No. 3, a unique and remarkable Alco A-class Atlantic, here downgraded and shabby in local service, May 1949.

No. 153, class F3 Pacific built in 1910, leaves Wauwatosa, Wisconsin in 1947.

No. 152, class F3-cs built by American Locomotive in 1910 and streamlined in 1941 for *Chippewa Hiawatha* service. It entered service as No. 1542; became No. 3240 in June 1910; No. 6540 in 1912; No. 6160 in 1924; No. 152 in 1938, and was scrapped in 1954.

No. 5930, a gas-electric, pulling a single coach car between Milwaukee and Janesville, June 1949.

No. 8, a Fairbanks-Morse 6,000 horsepower, three-unit locomotive, the *Olympian Hiawatha Special*.

Clearing tracks, circa 1949. No. 983 was a RSC-2 diesel built by American Locomotive.

Diesel No. 5900, half-locomotive half-baggage car built in the company shops. Photographed on the run between Milwaukee and Berlin, Wisconsin, June 1950.

No. 991, RSC-2 diesel built by American Locomotive, operating between Minocqua and Lisbon, Wisconsin, October 1949.

No. 1119, class G6S built by Baldwin in 1900, photographed June 1951. Two months later, this engine was scrapped.

No. 707, class L2, photographed June 1951. Three months later, this engine was scrapped.

Locomotives No. 144 and No. 140, two class F-6A workhorses, photographed in 1950.

Locomotive No. 1412, class I5A switch engine, photographed April 1953.

No. 98-C, an EMD FP-7, pulling the *Hiawatha* along the Mississippi en route to the Twin Cities, 1953.

Super Dome in the Wisconsin Dells.

A five-alarm fire caused $325,000 damage at the Menomonee River Valley roundhouse, February 28, 1957. *Milwaukee Journal* photo.

No 19-B, an EMD E7 built in 1946, sporting Union Pacific colors as adopted in 1955. Photographed September 16, 1958. *Milwaukee Journal* photo.

A three-unit diesel locomotive with EMD FP7 A-unit at Palmyra, Wisconsin, circa-1960.

The same train as pictured opposite moves through the Wisconsin countryside.

The Iconografix Photo Archive Series includes:

AMERICAN CULTURE

AMERICAN SERVICE STATIONS 1935-1943	ISBN 1-882256-27-1
COCA-COLA: A HISTORY IN PHOTOGRAPHS 1930-1969	ISBN 1-882256-46-8
COCA-COLA: ITS VEHICLES IN PHOTOGRAPHS 1930-1969	ISBN 1-882256-47-6
PHILLIPS 66 1945-1954	ISBN 1-882256-42-5

AUTOMOTIVE

IMPERIAL 1955-1963	ISBN 1-882256-22-0
IMPERIAL 1964-1968	ISBN 1-882256-23-9
LE MANS 1950: THE BRIGGS CUNNINGHAM CAMPAIGN	ISBN 1-882256-21-2
PACKARD MOTOR CARS 1935-1942	ISBN 1-882256-44-1
PACKARD MOTOR CARS 1946-1958	ISBN 1-882256-45-X
SEBRING 12-HOUR RACE 1970	ISBN 1-882256-20-4
STUDEBAKER 1933-1942	ISBN 1-882256-24-7
STUDEBAKER 1946-1958	ISBN 1-882256-25-5
LINCOLN MOTOR CARS 1920-1942	ISBN 1-882256-57-3
LINCOLN MOTOR CARS 1946-1960	ISBN 1-882256-58-1
MG 1945-1964	ISBN 1-882256-52-2
MG 1965-1980	ISBN 1-882256-53-0

TRACTORS AND CONSTRUCTION EQUIPMENT

CASE TRACTORS 1912-1959	ISBN 1-882256-32-8
CATERPILLAR MILITARY TRACTORS VOLUME 1	ISBN 1-882256-16-6
CATERPILLAR MILITARY TRACTORS VOLUME 2	ISBN 1-882256-17-4
CATERPILLAR SIXTY	ISBN 1-882256-05-0
CATERPILLAR THIRTY	ISBN 1-882256-04-2
CLETRAC AND OLIVER CRAWLERS	ISBN 1-882256-43-3
FARMALL F-SERIES	ISBN 1-882256-02-6
FARMALL MODEL H	ISBN 1-882256-03-4
FARMALL MODEL M	ISBN 1-882256-15-8
FARMALL REGULAR	ISBN 1-882256-14-X

FARMALL SUPER SERIES	ISBN 1-882256-49-2
FORDSON 1917-1928	ISBN 1-882256-33-6
HART-PARR	ISBN 1-882256-08-5
HOLT TRACTORS	ISBN 1-882256-10-7
INTERNATIONAL TRACTRACTOR	ISBN 1-882256-48-4
JOHN DEERE MODEL A	ISBN 1-882256-12-3
JOHN DEERE MODEL B	ISBN 1-882256-01-8
JOHN DEERE MODEL D	ISBN 1-882256-00-X
JOHN DEERE 30 SERIES	ISBN 1-882256-13-1
MINNEAPOLIS-MOLINE U-SERIES	ISBN 1-882256-07-7
OLIVER TRACTORS	ISBN 1-882256-09-3
RUSSELL GRADERS	ISBN 1-882256-11-5
TWIN CITY TRACTOR	ISBN 1-882256-06-9

RAILWAYS

GREAT NORTHERN RAILWAY 1945-1970	ISBN 1-882256-56-5
MILWAUKEE ROAD 1850-1960	ISBN 1-882256-61-1

TRUCKS

BEVERAGE TRUCKS 1910-1975	ISBN 1-882256-60-3
BROCKWAY TRUCKS 1948-1961	ISBN 1-882256-55-7
DODGE TRUCKS 1929-1947	ISBN 1-882256-36-0
DODGE TRUCKS 1948-1960	ISBN 1-882256-37-9
LOGGING TRUCKS 1915-1970	ISBN 7-882256-59-X
MACK MODEL AB	ISBN 1-882256-18-2
MACK AP SUPER DUTY TRKS 1926-1938	ISBN 1-882256-54-9
MACK MODEL B 1953-1966 VOLUME 1	ISBN 1-882256-19-0
MACK MODEL B 1953-1966 VOLUME 2	ISBN 1-882256-34-4
MACK EB-EC-ED-EE-EF-EG-DE 1936-1951	ISBN 1-882256-29-8
MACK EH-EJ-EM-EQ-ER-ES 1936-1950	ISBN 1-882256-39-5
MACK FC-FCSW-NW 1936-1947	ISBN 1-882256-28-X
MACK FG-FH-FJ-FK-FN-FP-FT-FW 1937-1950	ISBN 1-882256-35-2
MACK LF-LH-LJ-LM-LT 1940-1956	ISBN 1-882256-38-7
STUDEBAKER TRUCKS 1927-1940	ISBN 1-882256-40-9
STUDEBAKER TRUCKS 1941-1964	ISBN 1-882256-41-7

The Iconografix Photo Archive Series is available from direct mail specialty book dealers and bookstores worldwide, or can be ordered from the publisher. For additional information or to add your name to our mailing list contact:

Iconografix
PO Box 609/BK
Osceola, Wisconsin 54020 USA

Telephone: (715) 294-2792
(800) 289-3504 (USA)
Fax: (715) 294-3414

Book trade distribution by Voyageur Press, Inc., PO Box 338, Stillwater, Minnesota 55082 USA (800) 888-9653
European distribution by Midland Publishing Limited, 24 The Hollow, Earl Shilton, Leicester LE9 7N1 England

MORE GREAT BOOKS FROM ICONOGRAFIX

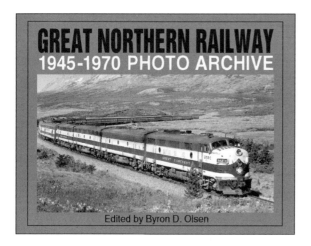

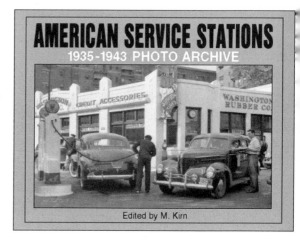

GREAT NORTHERN RAILWAY 1945-1970 *Photo Archive* ISBN 1-882256-56-5

AMERICAN SERVICE STATIONS 1935-1943 *Photo Archive* ISBN 1-882256-27-1

COCA-COLA: ITS VEHICLES IN PHOTOGRAPHS 1930-1969 *Photo Archive* ISBN 1-882256-47-6

MACK MODEL B 1953-1966 VOLUME 1 *Photo Archive* ISBN 1-882256-19-0

OLIVER TRACTORS *Photo Archive* ISBN 1-882256-09-3

LOGGING TRUCKS 1915-1970 *Photo Archive* ISBN 1-882256-59-X

CATERPILLAR SIXTY *Photo Archive* ISBN 1-882256-05-0

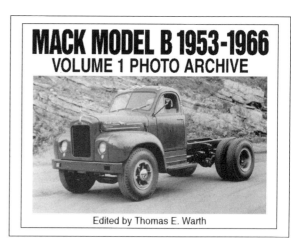

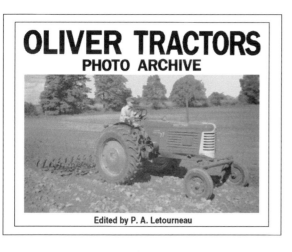

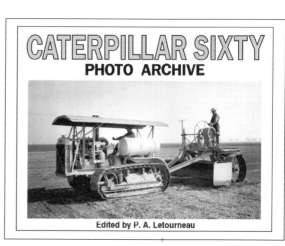